TAYLOR SWIFT

TAYLOR SWIFT

FIONA STERLING

CONTENTS

Disclaimer

The content of this book is intended for informational and entertainment purposes only. While every effort has been made to ensure the accuracy and reliability of the information provided, the author and publisher assume no responsibility for errors, omissions, or inaccuracies. The opinions expressed herein are solely those of the author and do not necessarily reflect the views of the subjects or their representatives.

This book is not endorsed, authorized, or affiliated with any of the individuals, organizations, or companies mentioned. All information about the public figures discussed in this book is based on publicly available sources, and no proprietary or confidential information has been used.

Any resemblance to real persons, living or dead, is purely coincidental, and the author and publisher disclaim any liability for any direct, indirect, incidental, or consequential damage arising from the use of the information in this book. Readers are encouraged to conduct their own research and verify any information provided.

By reading this book, you agree to hold the author and publisher harmless from any claims, damages, or liabilities arising from its use.

CHAPTER 2

Introduction

Taylor Swift was born on December 13, 1989, and while she may have been born in Pennsylvania, she was raised in Nashville, Tennessee. As a child she wanted to become a singer and at the same time her parents returned to their roots in Pennsylvania to work at their Christmas tree farm. Raised in the heart of the country music business in the music capital of the south, she began singing at the age of eleven and landed her first record label by the time she turned the majority age of eighteen. Always in a family of great means, they raised Taylor to know the value of money and to always work hard to gain what she wanted. When Taylor was playing the role of Ethel Peas in Maine (a stage play debut for Taylor) she fell for the son of Robert Kennedy Jr., and two carried on a love affair. Because Taylor and Connor were always on the road, they broke up in 2012.

Taylor Swift is best known as a pop sensation who has reinvented herself and who has a large portfolio of records, showing diversity and many changes to her style. She is also well-known for not ending many of her personal relationships in peace, but rather taking to her pen to write and record songs venting about how she was treated by those in the relationship. This guide seeks to discover the different aspects of Taylor Swift's life and how they could create such honesty in her music.

Chapter 1: Early Life and Childhood Journey

'Hurricane Taylor' Taylor Swift was born on December 13th, 1989 in Reading, Pennsylvania. She was named after the famous singer James Taylor, who was known for his soulful melodies and captivating performances that left the audience in awe. Swift's parents, Andrea and Scott Swift, were immensely proud of their little bundle of joy and cherished her like a precious gift from above. Alongside her parents, she had a younger brother named Austin, whose contagious laughter and mischievous antics brought endless joy to their household. The Swift family embodied love, unity, and unwavering support for one another. Scott, a Merrill Lynch financial advisor, possessed a sharp business acumen and an incredible knack for managing finances. His expertise in the field allowed him to provide a secure and stable environment for his family. Meanwhile, Andrea, a former mutual fund marketing executive, possessed a remarkable blend of creativity and determination. Her passion for marketing and her innate ability to connect with people laid the foundation for her daughter's successful career in the music industry. In 1989, the Swift family decided to embark on a new chapter of their lives and moved to Wyomissing, Pennsylvania. This vibrant and close-knit community embraced the Swifts with open arms, laying the groundwork for the incredible journey that awaited the young Taylor. She enrolled at West Reading Elementary Center, where she showcased her boundless enthusiasm and love for learning. It was during these early years that she began to develop her distinctive voice and a fierce determination to achieve her dreams. Swift's childhood was a tapestry woven with moments of joy, exploration, and self-discovery. She delved into a myriad of hobbies and activities, always seeking to expand her horizons. One of her notable experiences was working in a bird sanctuary, where she witnessed the beauty of nature and developed a deep appreciation for its wonders. This connection with the natural world would later find its way into the heartfelt lyrics of her songs, which resonated with millions around the globe. Despite her vivacious spirit and passion for life, Swift encountered her fair share of challenges. One of the most poignant moments occurred when she was unable to accompany her beloved family on a trip to Disney World. Determined not to let her disappointment consume her, she and her brother, armed with an intricately drawn map, envisioned the adventures they would have experienced. However, fate intervened, and her mother broke the news that they would not be able to go. The disappointment was palpable, and Swift recalls this day as one of the toughest of her youth. It was a lesson in resilience, teaching her to appreciate the value of dreams and the tenacity required to pursue them. From these experiences, a seed began to grow within Swift's soul—a seed that would flourish into a lifelong passion for music. Her grandmother, a professional opera singer, paved the way, igniting Swift's deep admiration for the power of the human voice. At a tender age, her dreams nourished by her grandmother's legacy, Swift ventured to the awe-inspiring city of New York for vocal and acting lessons. Every weekend, she eagerly hopped into the family car beside her supportive parents and set off on the journey to Long Island, where her vocal talents would be nurtured. At the age of 10, Swift's voice soared through the halls of a Philadelphia 76ers basketball game, as she fearlessly sang the national anthem, capturing the hearts of the audience with her angelic tones. This extraordinary moment marked the dawn of a budding star, whose destiny was intertwined with the magic of music. At age 11, she graced the diamond of a Philadelphia Phillies baseball game, performing a breathtaking rendition of "The Star-Spangled Banner." Her captivating presence and soul-stirring vocals left the crowd spellbound, foreshadowing the mesmerizing performances that awaited her in the years to come. Swift's passion for music would not be contained within the realm of her vocals alone. At the age of 12, she embarked on a journey to master the guitar, inspired by the enduring melodies and emotional depth that only this instrument could provide. It was an unconventional path to music mastery, as she observed a computer repairman skillfully mending her family's device. Intrigued by the intricacies of the guitar, Swift's curiosity led her to acquire the basics, learning three chords that would later set her on a path to musical greatness. As the tender age of thirteen enveloped her, Swift found solace in the art of songwriting. She deftly penned her first verse and chorus to a heartfelt tune titled "Lucky You", pouring her emotions onto the page like ink from an open well. It was a cathartic experience, an expression of her innermost thoughts and an awakening of her innate songwriting talent. During a fateful visit to the theater to witness a stellar production of "Les Misérables," Swift was captivated by the magic unfolding on stage. She turned to her parents, her eyes sparkling with inspiration, and resolutely declared that this was her calling. From that moment forward, the world became her stage, and Swift embarked on a transformative journey that would lead her to become one of the most influential and beloved artists of her generation.

In the depths of her heart, Swift knew that her destiny was intertwined with music. The melodies that streamed effortlessly from her soul traversed genres and touched the hearts of millions worldwide. With each note, she forged an unbreakable connection, uniting individuals across continents, transcending language barriers, and evoking emotions that only music can evoke. In the bustling city streets, amidst the whirlwind of lights and a cacophony of sounds, a superstar was born. 'Hurricane Taylor' Swift was set to sweep the world, leaving a trail of mesmerized audiences, shattered records, and heartfelt anthems in her wake.

Family Background

Taylor Alison Swift was born in Reading, Pennsylvania on December 13, 1989. She grew up in nearby Wyomissing, Pennsylvania. The oldest of two children, Swift has a younger brother named Austin. Her mother, Andrea Swift, was a homemaker who had worked as a mutual fund marketing executive before having children. Her father, Scott Kingsley Swift, was a stockbroker for Merrill Lynch; the family's Christmas tree farm provided additional income. Taylor Swift enjoys quoting the old adage that you can take the girl out of the country, but you can't take the country out of the girl. "I am the only person in my family to have been born in a hospital. I certainly should have been born on the side of a valley," she told in 2011. She learned to ride horses before she could walk and spent her weekdays at a private Christian school, where she made friends with the daughters of local Amish families. "I grew up on an actual working Christmas tree farm," Swift said. "We had a pickup truck and a welcome," she would add during her concerts. Swift was fascinated by country music and her parents indulged her early interest with a vault of albums. She absorbed the music of Patsy Cline, Dolly Parton, and her own idols, the Dixie Chicks. By age

10, Swift was entering contests in suburban Philadelphia that were stocked with kid dancers and non-threatening pre-teens with guitars. When those early attempts at stardom failed, Taylor and her mom began making regular business trips to Nashville to build her career. When Swift was 11, the family started spending extended weekends in the country music capital. For two years, they stayed at the Comfort Suites. Swift and her mom were a two-girl band, the diminutive singer crooning Elvis covers, the six-foot-tall Andrea commanding the Yamaha mini-disk player. Taylor's dedication and passion for country music only grew stronger as she continued her musical journey. Her talent and distinctive voice soon caught the attention of music executives and she was offered a recording contract. This marked the beginning of Swift's skyrocketing success in the music industry. With each album release, she captivated audiences worldwide, winning numerous awards, including multiple Grammy Awards. Swift's songwriting skills also gained widespread acclaim, with her heartfelt and relatable lyrics resonating with millions of fans. Alongside her incredible music career, Taylor Swift is also known for her philanthropic efforts. She has generously donated to various charitable causes, supporting education, disaster relief, and social justice initiatives. Despite her immense fame, Swift remains grounded and actively engages with her fanbase, often sharing personal moments and insights through social media. Swift's impact on popular culture is undeniable, as she continues to break records, push boundaries, and inspire aspiring musicians around the globe. Her authenticity, talent, and unwavering determination have solidified her status as one of the most influential artists of her generation. As Taylor Swift continues to evolve as an artist, her fans eagerly await her future endeavors and eagerly anticipate the next chapter in her extraordinary career.

Musical Influences

According to the artist herself, some of Taylor Swift's early childhood inspirations in music came from being exposed to early country music acts such as Dolly Parton, Shania Twain, Faith Hill, Tim McGraw, Lonestar, and even LeAnn Rimes. She was fifteen and recorded her first demos in 2002 with a deal with RCA Records in the works when Scott Borchetta of Big Machine Records discovered her and promptly signed the young artist. Her self-titled first album in 2006 featured multiple pop instruments, including strings and a heavy piano, and would go on to earn the Best New Female Vocalist Award in 2007 from the Academy of Country Music. At the 2009 Grammy Awards, she took home four awards, including Album of the Year. She even collaborated with John Mayer on "Half of My Heart", a song that made it to John's Battle Studies album and to number 2 on the Adult Pop Chart in 2010. Although her first love was country, Swift felt she would be less likely to meet her idols due to the distance and lower rate of travel in the UK, and slipped instead to the sounds of British singer-songwriters like Imogen Heap, Coldplay, Snow Patrol, and her favorite, Remus Lupins. According to REM Lazarus in his biography of the artist, Coldplay was particularly comforting and close to her Americana-oriented sensibilities. Her exposure in the UK to this variety of pop sounds, in which show voices navigated the production, was a critical half of her musical makeup. While she was not attempting to sing the big-voice belting of Maria Callas, Céline Dion, or Whitney Houston, on whom many pop idols modeled, Swift was also uninterested in imitating Britney Spears or Christina Aguilera. Accidentally, she became legible to a different set of listeners due to this orientation. Her vocal emotivity shared some values with Alanis Morissette and Sheryl Crow, less arch 1970s Carly Simon and Joni Mitchell. As her career continued to flourish, Taylor Swift ventured into new musical territories, experimenting with different genres and collaborating with a diverse range of artists. Her growth as an artist was evident in her later albums, which showcased her versatility and ability to seamlessly incorporate various musical elements into her songs. With each new release, Swift continued to captivate audiences with her heartfelt lyrics, relatable storytelling, and infectious melodies. She became a global sensation, breaking numerous records and defying expectations along the way. Today, Taylor Swift stands as one of the most successful and influential musicians of her generation, with a massive fan base and a legacy that will undoubtedly leave a lasting impact on the music industry.

Chapter 2: Rise to Fame

As a gifted and talented country artist, Taylor Swift effortlessly propelled herself into the realm of music icons at a remarkably young age, captivating audiences worldwide with the release of her very first album and a string of chart-topping singles. Swift's music is undeniably a heartfelt exploration of the intricacies of love and relationships, resonating deeply with fans and critics alike. She has garnered a tremendous following, boasting millions of devoted admirers around the globe. Drawing both praise and critique, Taylor Swift's musical prowess has been recognized and honored by various prestigious organizations, showering her with countless prestigious awards. While Taylor Swift's musical achievements continue to soar, her dedicated fans eagerly anticipate her transcendence into the realms of film and television, eagerly awaiting the day when she graces the silver screen and small screen alike with her immense talent. Back in 2006, the world was captivated by the rise of Taylor Swift when she boldly introduced herself to the music scene with her debut album. The infectious charm of "Tim McGraw," the first single from her eponymous album, struck a resounding chord with audiences, catapulting her into the commercial and radio spheres as an undisputed sensation. Not content with just one hit, Taylor Swift delighted fans with a string of successful singles, including the lovesick ballad "Teardrops on My Guitar," the irresistibly catchy "Our Song," the fiery declaration of independence in "Picture to Burn," and the defiant anthem of "Should've Said No." Such was their popularity that the US version of Swift's album achieved a remarkable milestone, certified as triple-platinum by the RIAA after selling over 2.5 million copies. Garnering widespread acclaim, "Taylor Swift" debuted at an impressive number 19 on the revered Billboard 200 chart, holding its position for a staggering 157 weeks. As of July 2021, the album has globally sold a staggering 7.51 million copies, solidifying its status as the most successful production album of the 21st century, delivering an incredible eight unforgettable singles that continue to captivate audiences worldwide. 2016 marked another pivotal moment in Taylor Swift's career with the release of her album "Fearless." This awe-inspiring masterpiece rapidly ascended to the summit of the coveted Billboard 200, dominating the chart for an impressive eleven consecutive weeks. Within its first week, "Fearless" triumphantly achieved sales of a remarkable 592,304 copies, illustrating the unrivaled appeal of Swift's musical prowess. The album's supremacy extended beyond the realm of country as it soared to number one on the revered Top Country Albums chart, where it maintained an impressive reign for a phenomenal 86 nonconsecutive weeks. Swift's remarkable achievement also etched her name in music history, as she became the first artist since the Beatles to debut two number one albums within a span of less than a year on this prestigious chart. Furthermore, "Fearless" joins an esteemed lineup of only ten albums that have spent a minimum of eleven weeks at the helm of the charts since Nielsen SoundScan introduced its revolutionary tracking system back in 1991. Expanding her diverse musical portfolio, Taylor Swift welcomed the enchanting voices of Colbie Caillat and B.o.B to collaborate on a delightful holiday EP titled "Soundtrack 1," released in December 2007. Leaving an indelible mark on the music industry, the EP immediately made its grand entrance at number one, captivating listeners with its infectious melodies and captivating lyrics.

Debut Album: Taylor Swift

In October 2006, the immensely talented and prodigious artist Taylor Swift embarked on her musical journey with the release of her awe-inspiring and highly anticipated debut album, aptly titled "Taylor Swift." The magnitude of its impact on both critics and audiences alike exceeded all expectations, propelling it to the remarkable achievement of securing the fifth position on the prestigious Billboard 200. The album's extraordinary success continued to soar as it mesmerized the hearts of music enthusiasts, astonishingly selling a staggering 5.24 million copies within the United States alone. One of the mesmerizing ballads from this exceptional album, "Tim McGraw," effortlessly soared into the upper echelons of the renowned Billboard Hot 100, captivating listeners worldwide. Recognizing its undeniable brilliance, the Recording Industry Association of America (RIAA) awarded this masterpiece with a platinum certification. Swift's ingenious artistry did not stop there, as her subsequent singles such as the enchanting "Teardrops on My Guitar" and the melodious "Our Song" conquered the charts, ascending to the pinnacle of success and earning countless multi-platinum accolades. Despite encountering various challenges, including limited airplay on country radio for "Tim McGraw" and some of her subsequent singles, Taylor Swift's dedication and sheer talent amassed an unwavering and extensive fan base. The overwhelming support bolstered her meteoric rise to stardom, aided by the groundbreaking success of her MySpace page and the remarkable feat of self-publishing thousands of downloads on the acclaimed platform, iTunes. Swift's undeniable talent and online presence acted as the catalyst for her signing with the esteemed independent record label, Big Machine Records, forever changing the course of her illustrious career. Years later, the profound impact of Taylor Swift's eponymous debut album on Big Machine Records continues to reverberate through the annals of music history, solidifying its status as the "cornerstone release" of the label's first ever decade, as proclaimed by the reputable Billboard. Its seminal role was instrumental in establishing Big Machine Records as a force to be reckoned with in the music industry. Furthermore, Taylor Swift stands triumphant as the first artist in recent history to have a debut album, bearing her own name, penetrate the illustrious Top 40 since the indelible LeAnn Rimes achieved this milestone with her iconic release, "Blue," back in the monumental year of 1996. Elevating the notion of supremacy to unprecedented heights, the magnificence of Taylor Swift's inaugural masterpiece reigned supreme as the best-selling album within the United States for an astounding span of 20 weeks. Its unyielding popularity and timeless appeal ensured its enduring presence on the charts, holding firm for an awe-inspiring 157 consecutive weeks. To this day, "Taylor Swift" proudly retains its place on the hallowed all-time chart in the United States, standing tall at an impressive number 15 for the most weeks spent captivating the hearts and minds of music enthusiasts nationwide.

Breakthrough Success: Fearless

Some of the time spent in the studio for creating Taylor Swift's self-titled album was used writing and recording songs for her second album. Taylor Swift's second studio album, Fearless, was released on November 11 and debuted at number one on the Billboard 200. The album, promoted by singles such as 'Love Story,' 'You Belong With Me,' and 'Fifteen,' achieved commercial and critical success according to something that few others could imagine for a country artist. The album debuted with 592,304 paid downloads in its first week, the highest number for a country album since they first began tracking digital download sales in 2004. Fearless debuted at No. 1 in the United States and generated sales of 129 million songs. The album sold 7,145,000 units, reached the top of the charts in 11 countries, and sold 8,681,000 singles. Fearless won the Grammy Award for Album of the Year and Best Country Album at the 52nd Grammy Awards on January 31st, 2010. The Academy of Country Music awarded the album with the Album of the Year in 2009 and another Female-Vocalist of the Year nod. Taylor Swift wrote seven of it, some on her bedroom floor at home, and collaborated with co-writers Liz Rose, Hillary Lindsey, Colbie Caillat, and John Rich on others. The album is still on the Billboard 200 after more than 150 weeks and has topped the pop and country charts. In mid-November 2008, Fearless topped iTunes's sales. Sources say that Swift has tested 5 or 6 new tracks and that plans for a reissue are in the works. Acclaimed by teenage critics as one of the most significant aspects of Fearless is the friendly, youthful celebrity behind the makeup who gives it a typically down-to-earth twist in her acceptance speeches. Fans see a friendliness and personal attention to performing live, known by notes and performances on sites such as MySpace and YouTube. Critical response 'Fearless' received numerous awards and predominantly positive feedback from critics. Things like songwriting style or vocal delivery, as well as the use of "real" instruments have been recognized by country music websites as reflective of less-youthful artists in the genre. Vogue magazine hailed Swift as the "Anti-Britney" in its review. Lynch and Finn have speculated that a farewell dismissal of this most recent review is a resonation of Fearless's marketing as "a sleek, expensive artifact in the Disney pop machine." Swift, who is also promoted by Wal-Mart, was expected to receive radio pay for Fearless. Popular culture and affect Musically, Fearless explores the hit 'You Belong With Me,' other typically country varieties such as roots music and classic rock. Things like songwriting style or vocal delivery, as well as the use of "real" instruments have been recognized by country music websites as reflective of less-youthful artists in the genre. Vogue magazine hailed Swift as the "Anti-Britney" in its review. Lynch and Finn have speculated that a farewell dismissal of this most recent review is a resonation of Fearless's marketing as "a sleek, expensive artifact in the Disney pop machine." There have been cultural consequences for their fan base, which has included Googling "Beyoncé," leading it to the #1 trend on the website. "Now who is that waiting to get her fifteen minutes?" asks Swift in her acceptance speech. "I LOVE Taylor Swift She May Have Been a Surprise but I Thought She Deserved the Awards for 'Fifteen' That's My Song To Life !!!!" The Daily Show host Jon Stewart asked whether he was a fan of Swift. Swift appeared on The Ellen DeGeneres Show to promote Fearless and perform 'Change,' her newest song. In September 2007, after performing the song at a fashion depot event, Swift declared that she wore her pied piper's headband in order to connect with her fans and show her appreciation for their support.

CHAPTER 5

Chapter 3: Musical Evolution

Taylor's musical style has undergone significant changes since her early days as a country singer-songwriter. It is not only her music that has evolved, but her entire public image. While there are still some resemblances, there is no doubt that Taylor, along with her music, has completely transformed as we approach the release of her ninth studio album. During her initial four records, Taylor was undeniably a country artist. Drawing inspiration from her own love and relationship experiences, she crafted songs that were sometimes authentic and sometimes exaggerated in their storytelling. In those early years of her music career, she exhibited vulnerability, anger, and playfulness, which led to immense success both within and beyond the boundaries of country music. However, her trajectory took a turn with "Red," signifying a shift in her style. Gradually, she became more adaptable, leaving behind her innocent image for a darker and edgier persona. Though traces of country elements were still visible in her new sound, the incorporation of pop stylings allowed her to break free from her previous mold and solidify her popularity. It was "Shake It Off" that truly encapsulated Taylor's transformative journey. She completely let go of her country roots and fully embraced the synthpop genre, boldly announcing that she would brush off all the criticism and setbacks she had faced in the preceding years. With her notable contributions to collaborative works, Taylor's name seemed to be everywhere, and her music became inescapable. Her public persona faded into the background, giving way to the emergence of Reputation-era Taylor, characterized by brooding aesthetics, dark hair, and an attitude of defiance. The release of "Look What You Made Me Do" marked a return to her angry style, but it wasn't long before Taylor reverted to her true self with heartfelt tracks like "Delicate" and "New Year's Day." Now, with "Lover," Taylor explores and celebrates love in its various forms. Whether it's romantic love, love for her friends, or love for herself, this album is a testament to the beauty of loving relationships. Taylor's journey has taken her through a diverse range of styles, showcasing her growth and artistic versatility. She has proven time and time again that she is not afraid to take risks and reinvent herself. As she enters this new chapter of her career, fans can only anticipate the remarkable evolution that Taylor will continue to embark upon, as she constantly pushes the boundaries of her own creativity.

Transition to Pop Music

Transition to Pop Music Initially, Swift's move from country music to pop music was deemed a perilous decision due to the risk of alienating the vast number of country music enthusiasts she had cultivated throughout her career. However, her groundbreaking first official single from the album "1989," titled "Shake It Off," defied all expectations and catapulted to the summit of the prestigious Billboard Hot 100 chart. This momentous achievement marked the dawning of Swift's new era in pop music, accompanied by a transformation in her iconic image. She fearlessly bid farewell to her signature long, flowing curls and embraced a chic, shorter, straight hairdo, signifying her evolution as an artist. In recognition of her immense impact on the music world, Billboard bestowed upon Taylor Swift the title of New York City's Global Welcome Ambassador in 2014. The highly anticipated release of "1989" on October 27, 2014, solidified her position as a force to be reckoned with in the pop music landscape. True to her staggering popularity, the album instantaneously soared to the top of the Billboard 200 chart, astonishingly accumulating over 800,000 pre-orders alone. By early 2015, Taylor Swift had amassed an extraordinary repertoire of accomplishments, boasting an impressive twelve top 40 singles hits, including a remarkable four chart-toppers on the coveted Hot 100. Additionally, she had secured six prestigious Grammy Awards and an astounding eleven American Music Awards, further illustrating the unparalleled success of her transition from country music to pop. Swift's ability to captivate and enthrall audiences across diverse musical genres attested to her unmatched appeal and talent, cementing her status as an unparalleled musical prodigy. When Taylor Swift released her game-changing single "Shake It Off," excitement rippled through the music industry. Good Morning America anchor, Amy Robach, reported that contrary to initial concerns that Swift might face a decline in fan base, the multi-talented artist experienced a surge in popularity with each passing day, captivating countless new fans. Consequently, any apprehension regarding her loss of credibility by venturing into pop music proved unfounded. A discerning Los Angeles Times writer astutely observed that Swift's remarkable journey mirrored the narrative of her own songs — a small-town girl fearlessly pursuing her dreams in the metropolis and attracting widespread acclaim. Swift's transition to pop music not only marked a pivotal moment in her career but also demonstrated her ability to innovate and captivate audiences across boundaries. It served as a testament to her unwavering passion for music and her unparalleled talent, cementing her legacy as one of the most influential and versatile artists of our time.

Reputation and Lover Era

Reputation Era (November 2017 – March 2018) Before the release of Reputation, Swift disappeared from public attention, leaving her fans eagerly awaiting her return. Her absence from social media was only punctuated by the occasional enigmatic glimpses of a snake, a symbol that captivated the curiosity of her dedicated followers. The serpent, a potent metaphor for danger and deceit in the celebrity world, quickly became the subject of intense speculation and interpretation. What seemed like an insult to some was seized by her devoted fans, who proudly brandished snake signs at her tour shows, reclaiming the symbol as a badge of honor. As Reputation finally graced the world with its presence, it brought forth a collection of songs that delved deep into the tumultuous yet fascinating experience of being in the public eye. With anticipation bubbling over, two singles from the album, namely "...Ready for It?" on September 3 and "Gorgeous" on October 20, were unveiled to give fans a tantalizing taste of what was yet to come. After the album's release, Swift embarked on a series of secret listening sessions, providing her loyal supporters with an exclusive opportunity to explore the intricate meanings woven into each track. Among these revelations, she described the enchanting "Delicate" as a heartfelt ode to "falling in love with someone who makes your life feel lovelier." These intimate conversations added an extra layer of intimacy and connection between the artist and her fervent audience. True to its title, Reputation soared to the top of the charts, solidifying Swift's status as a musical powerhouse. The album achieved the remarkable feat of selling one million copies in the United States alone, joining the ranks of a select few albums to achieve such a tremendous milestone since 2014. Its success not only confirmed Swift's enduring popularity but also marked a pivotal moment in her artistic evolution. Having grown weary of the personas and theatrical costumes that had defined her earlier works, Swift fearlessly stepped into a new era with Reputation. To the pleasant surprise of her fans, the record revealed that the "Old Taylor" was very much alive and well. This new chapter in her musical journey explored darker themes than ever before, chronicling the ebbs and flows of relationships in their rawest, most vulnerable form. In essence, Reputation (2017) stood as a testament to Swift's unyielding resolve and determination to define herself amidst a sea of conflicting narratives. The protagonist in these powerful songs was acutely aware of her own identity, yet struggled relentlessly against the relentless tide of stories woven by others. Through her music, Swift invited her audience to join her on an introspective journey, unearthing the truths and vulnerabilities that lay hidden beneath the surface.

CHAPTER 6

Chapter 4: Impact and Influence

In just 13 short years, Taylor Swift has risen to become an incomparable force that demands recognition. As one of the most exceptionally successful musical artists in the entire United States, she has masterfully constructed an unshakeable musical empire that resonates with countless souls. Her impact extends far beyond the realm of music, capturing the attention of people from all walks of life. Every word she utters carries immense weight, even permeating the world of politics, where her influence is so profound that it commands attention. In a remarkable twist of fate, a mere hint of political support from Swift in 2018 sent shockwaves throughout her devoted fanbase, leaving thousands astounded by her power. It seems that whatever Swift does or says, the world is compelled to take notice, as if under a trance. Within the pages of this captivating chapter, we delve deep into the vast array of areas in which Swift leaves an indelible mark, leaving no doubt about her substantial impact. Harnessing the extraordinary power of her music and iconic image, Swift fearlessly champions messages of self-worth and empowerment. Her songs, far beyond being mere anthems of heartbreak and resilience, radiate with an unwavering focus on strength, resonating with individuals from every walk of life. Notably, certain music videos such as "The Man" explicitly champion feminist ideals, serving as overt and resounding declarations of Swift's unwavering support for gender equality. Yet, her influence stretches even further. Swift's unwavering commitment to making a difference extends to her tireless philanthropy, as she generously donates to numerous organizations and causes, striving to effect positive change within society. She is not solely an exceptionally talented musician but also an undeniable force of activism, exemplifying unwavering dedication to advocating for what she believes in. At the very moment this book came to fruition, Swift's name was once again plastered across headlines, as she fearlessly spearheaded a groundbreaking movement to secure a more favorable contract for fellow music artists. Despite encountering resistance from some within the industry, she received overwhelming support from countless individuals who recognized the dire need for change. Swift's astounding musical prowess extends well beyond traditional boundaries, permeating diverse platforms and transcending language barriers. Over the course of her prolific career, Swift has unleashed a stunning collection of over a dozen albums, captivating audiences worldwide with her compelling artistry. Her singles have skyrocketed to the top of global music charts, leaving an undeniable mark on the very fabric of musical history. Ever the trailblazer, Swift has ventured into the realm of online content, gracing YouTube with her mesmerizing music videos, capturing the hearts of her eager followers in breathtaking fashion. What may seem like a seemingly simple act of appearing or disappearing from various social media platforms creates a whirlwind of headlines, showcasing the immense impact she holds over her devoted fanbase. Swift's influence refuses to be contained within the confines of the music industry alone, as she effortlessly transcends boundaries and leaves an indelible imprint on society at large. She has shattered records and etched her name into the annals of history as both a groundbreaking musician and a fervent defender of social causes. Her clothing line stands as a testament to her multifaceted empire, a multimillion-dollar endeavor that effortlessly intertwines with and influences nearly every facet of our culture. The remarkable journey of Taylor Swift is one that cannot be encapsulated in mere words, as her power and influence continue to evolve and shape the very fabric of our society. Her impact extends far beyond her musical prowess, weaving an intricate tapestry of empowerment, social change, and unwavering dedication to making a difference. As we delve into the depths of her extraordinary story, the true magnitude of her influence becomes even more awe-inspiring, solidifying her irrefutable status as a force to be reckoned with.

Empowerment and Feminism

Empowerment and Feminism: Swift's Enduring Impact on the Advocacy for Women's Rights Swift's songs and statements serve as powerful testaments to her unwavering commitment to feminism and the promotion of women's rights. When questioned about the extent of her feminist efforts, Swift passionately expressed her desire to foster a culture where feminism no longer carries a negative stigma, emphasizing that it should be a "no-brainer" to advocate for gender equality. While she acknowledges that she hasn't fully grasped every aspect of feminism, Swift remains dedicated to empowering women and dismantling societal barriers. Above all, Swift treasures the acceptance and endorsement she receives from fellow feminists. She recognizes the vitality of the ever-evolving third-wave feminists, who embrace diverse ways of identifying with feminism. In addition to her activism, Swift's songs themselves embody the spirit of female empowerment. Countless female fans have attested that her poignant lyrics have become anthems for themselves and their friends, resonating deeply with their personal journeys. By delving into the profound meaning within Swift's music, this section aims to explore the intricacies surrounding the construction and reception of the authenticity of feminism that permeates her artistry. The subsequent pages provide an in-depth analysis of how Swift has become a beacon of influence, shaping conversations on empowerment and feminism within her fanbase. Through her music, Swift contributes to the multifaceted discourse on these topics, adding depth and dimension to ongoing discussions. The sheer capacity of her fanbase to contemplate the profound connections between Swift's music and personal relationships speaks volumes about her cultural impact and significance. Moreover, her authentic performances of feminism and narratives of victimization can be seen as exemplifying Foucauldian strategies of conformity that both reflect and conform to contemporary narratives of empowerment. It is this unique ability that enables Swift to effortlessly embody the role of a malleable, mass-market-friendly feminist icon. Simultaneously aligning with the aspirations of her third-wave feminist base while appealing to a mainstream audience that may hold ambivalence or even hostility towards gender equity, Swift navigates the delicate balance between capital and protest. Within the realm of mass-market feminism discourse, she sparks discourse surrounding the inherent tensions within these spheres. Examining her role from a different perspective, Swift can also be viewed as an unparalleled symbol of empowerment, resilience, and resistance. In conclusion, Swift's enduring impact on the advocacy for women's rights cannot be underestimated. Her tireless dedication to feminism, both through her music and her public statements, continues to inspire countless individuals. By utilizing her platform to promote gender equality and challenge societal norms, Taylor Swift has cemented her place as an influential feminist icon, igniting conversations that will shape the future for generations to come.

Philanthropy and Activism

Philanthropy and Activism Swift has donated or raised millions of dollars for charity throughout her illustrious career. She has also wholeheartedly embraced her role as an advocate for positive change, continuously participating in various charity events and galvanizing support through her awe-inspiring performances. In a remarkable display of generosity, Swift pledged to donate significant portions of the proceeds from her astounding concert tours and the sales of her merchandise to an array of admirable charitable causes. Remarkably, Swift's philanthropic journey began in 2010 when she altruistically contributed $1 from each ticket sold for her spellbinding concerts to the charitable organization she was supporting at the time. This incredible act of benevolence exemplifies her unwavering commitment to touching lives and making a tangible difference. Among the numerous honorable causes that have been lifted by Swift's unwavering support are The American Red Cross, The Boys & Girls Club of America, Doctors Without Borders, Feeding America, MusiCares, NIH Children's Charities, The National Wildlife Federation, and the V Foundation for Cancer Research. The immeasurable impact she has had transcends monetary value, as her concerts and merchandise sales have combined to raise millions of dollars for these resolute charities, alongside many others that have been fortunate enough to receive her boundless support. Beyond her extraordinary monetary contributions, Swift has fervently devoted her time and radiant spirit to a myriad of charitable and social justice initiatives. In 2008, she selflessly donated $100,000 to help rescue the track and safeguard the invaluable youth programs at her beloved high school in Wyomissing, Pennsylvania. Not content with solely financial support, Swift has also delved into the realm of hands-on philanthropy, exemplified by her dedicated volunteer work at the esteemed New Jersey Salvation Army. Her unwavering commitment to improving the lives of others knows no bounds, as demonstrated by her remarkable $750,000 donation to the Salvation Army in April 2011. Moreover, Swift has used her influential platform to champion various aid efforts, wielding her enchanting voice to raise awareness and funds for crucial causes. Through the heartfelt release of her profound song "Ronan" for Stand Up to Cancer, Swift captivated hearts and invigorated a movement dedicated to eradicating this devastating disease. She has further displayed her unwavering compassion by supporting relief efforts during the West African Ebola outbreak and actively participating in disaster relief initiatives, most notably in Louisiana. The depth of Swift's philanthropic commitment is astounding, as she continuously demonstrates her determination to lend a helping hand to those in need. In 2016, she provided a poignant act of solidarity by donating a staggering $250,000 to assist Kesha in her protracted legal battles during the Sony trial. Swift's support extended even further in 2017 when she graciously gifted financial aid to two of her devoted fans in North America, ensuring that their holiday season was filled with joy and warmth. Additionally, in the face of the tumultuous COVID-19 outbreak, Swift once again stepped forward with unwavering empathy, donating $1,000 each to more than 30 individuals who tragically lost their income due to this unprecedented crisis. Swift's tireless efforts to make the world a better place through her philanthropy and activism exemplify her status not only as a revered artist but also as an unwavering champion for positive change. Her boundless generosity and dedication serve as an unwavering inspiration to us all, reminding us of the transformative power of compassion and unity.

Chapter 5: Personal Life

Personal Life Taylor Swift has been in the public eye since 2006, and the world has heard all about her music, her career, and various celebrity feuds or failed relationships. Swift is one of the few artists today who does not sweep her own personal life under the carpet. She is very open about her emotions, her love life, and her family. She is often spotted out with her never-ending list of celebrity BFFs and has had her public showdowns with famous enemies. Taylor Swift is someone we all feel like we know because she is so open and writes her music from the heart based on her own personal experiences. Taylor's fans are not the only ones privy to her personal life - the media has taken a keen interest in it also. Due to her public disputes with many of today's famous stars, the media have a field day reporting and speculating about everything Taylor does. In this chapter, the water gets a little deeper as we take a look at the Taylor Swifts and all the scandalous headlines, friends, family, and career turmoil. This chapter is a little more serious than the rest. Taylor has been through a lot of stuff, dating issues, and friendships that have fallen apart, and in addition to that, she has been betrayed by best friends and written about in the media. She has not had an easy time in the media, and she shares that she is bummed out if she cannot be pouty or cranky one day. As a result, she is fundamentally human.

Taylor Swift, the internationally acclaimed singer and songwriter, has captivated audiences worldwide with her incredible talent since her breakthrough in 2006. Throughout her illustrious career, she has garnered immense fame, not just for her remarkable music, but also for the intriguing details of her personal life that have unfolded before the public eye. Unlike many high-profile figures, Swift does not shy away from revealing her innermost emotions, intimate relationships, and cherished family bonds. She surrounds herself with a plethora of celebrity best friends, forming an unbreakable bond that the world can't help but envy. However, her journey is not without its challenges, as she has encountered public feuds with renowned stars, igniting a media frenzy that dissects her every move with undeniable fascination. In this chapter, we venture deeper into the enigmatic world of Taylor Swift, exploring the scandalous headlines, the intricate web of friends and family, and the turbulent twists and turns of her career. Step by step, we peel back the layers of her life, exposing her experiences with turbulent romantic entanglements and the unfortunate demise of once cherished friendships. The media too, plays an integral role in Taylor's life, diligently documenting her trials and triumphs as they cascade through the public consciousness. Amidst the intense scrutiny, Taylor remains resilient, bravely showcasing her vulnerability even when the weight of the world seems to rest upon her shoulders. While she stands as an idol to millions, Taylor Swift treats her fame with humility, remaining grounded in her humanity. Her emotions ebb and flow, and she allows herself to feel every shade of sadness or frustration that may come her way. After all, she is just like any other person, cherishing the simple joys, shouldering heartbreak, and striving to find her place in the world. Through her unwavering honesty and introspective songwriting, she connects with audiences on a level that goes beyond the superficial. Taylor Swift's personal journey echoes the collective human experience, reminding us that even amidst the brightest of spotlights, she is fundamentally, beautifully human.

Relationships and Public Image

Swift's relationships have often been the subject of intense media attention over the years. Ever since the highly-publicized Jessel-Michelle relationship, her personal life has subtly shaped public views of Swift in a way that continues to captivate audiences. "No matter how many Grammy Awards she wins, we will still be staring at those engagement fingers," exclaimed one tabloid headline, perfectly summarizing the constant fascination surrounding Swift's romantic endeavors. Swift's relationships have been thoroughly examined and analyzed in the book Swift: Celebrity, where her personal connections have been used to decipher the secrets behind her fame and success. As we delve into the intricate details of her past achievements, one thing becomes clear - at each stage of her personal relationships, the power dynamics are meticulously questioned and analyzed by fans and critics alike. It all began with her highly publicized romantic involvement with teen heartthrob Joe Jonas. Their relationship, however short-lived, left a lasting impact on Swift's career when it abruptly ended with a mere 27-second phone call. The phrase "27 seconds" quickly became a staple reference in once-popular YouTube fan videos, showcasing the strong connection between Swift's personal life and her dedicated fan base. Even though Swift often portrays herself as a hopeless romantic who co-writes passionate songs with her boyfriends, she subtly hinted at the breakdown of the relationship in the emotionally charged breakup anthem "Forever & Always". According to industry insiders and celebrity commentators, this particular relationship served as a catalyst for Swift's personal growth and artistic development. The subsequent public feud that followed their breakup undoubtedly influenced the three-month duration of their romantic involvement. Remarkably, this quantifiable measurement is evident through the extensive mentions and references found in kids' Glamour blog, indicating the immense public interest and fascination with Swift's rapid evolution during this period. In the case of Swift's relationship with actor Jake Gyllenhaal, things were less hostile but equally as drastic. The initial stages of Swift's high-profile romances hold an inexplicable and potent nostalgic value for her fans. During her music career peak and around the time of her collaboration on Calvin Harris' hit song "Summer," the gossip media fueled speculation about a potential "daydream engagement" between Swift and Harris. This pairing perfectly aligned with popular narratives of love and escapism, not only in terms of their domestic adventures and Swift's family holidays to Australia but also with Harris' unabashed show of affection through posing for a British tabloid while wearing Swift's "Pink Lady" jacket, oozing confidence and charm. However, it is crucial to acknowledge the symbolic gender dynamics present throughout their relationship. One adjective commonly used to describe Swift is "bossy," a label that was playfully assigned to her by Harris in a tweet. This incident took place even before their vacation to Australia, where Harris jokingly expressed his frustration about being "bossed around" by labels and the paparazzi. Furthermore, inspiration for their relationship can be found in the amalgamation of their shared musical tastes that became public knowledge. A Daily Mail article highlighted Swift's parents taking family pictures with the Harris family after a pleasant dinner in Beverly Hills. Additionally, a People cover story reported on Harris' attendance at one of Swift's concerts in Los Angeles, showcasing his unwavering hometown loyalty and further solidifying their bond. One particularly noteworthy relationship for Swift was her involvement with a pop boy-band singer known for his starkly different political views. The stark contrast between their politics, activist endeavors, and even fashion collaborations led to a riveting Swift narrative. The singer's unwavering support for Donald Trump was in direct opposition to Swift's efforts, resulting in an intriguing dichotomy. Throughout the duration of this relationship, a video unexpectedly surfaced, featuring Swift's mother accidentally pulling out a barbed wire fence in their Pennsylvania home while driving her two young daughters from school. This anecdote can be seen as reminiscent of the cherished Taylor Swift home movies often showcased during her concerts, further engaging and enchanting her loyal fan base. As the public obsession with Swift's personal life grew, she faced increased scrutiny for potentially positioning herself as an outsider in the industry, using her "debut" farm militia status and the acquisition of a significant amount of property to solidify her narrative. This scrutiny was briefly revisited in a thought-provoking article by the tabloid The Inquisitr and a satirical post on the blog "The Chive", both challenging the authenticity of her outsider image. Lastly, during her relationship with Harry Styles, a prominent member of the boy-band sensation One Direction, Swift and Styles were frequently compared to the legendary Hollywood couple Liz Taylor and Richard Burton. This striking parallel further fueled public interest and sparked numerous discussions in the media. In fact, during this period, a tabloid outlet called MediaTakeOut US even went so far as to dub Swift "Cray Cray", showcasing the undeniable impact that her romantic involvements have on public perception. Through all of these relationships and the accompanying media frenzy, one thing is certain - Taylor Swift's personal life has become an intricate part of her public persona. Her experiences, both joyful and heart-wrenching, have woven themselves into the fabric of her artistry, captivating audiences worldwide and leaving an indelible mark on her ever-evolving career.

Privacy and Media Attention

The importance of the divided focus in Swift's life helps to put this unique feature of her career into further perspective. Privacy is generally thought of in terms of the harm arising from media attention to an individual's right to be let alone. Swift has discussed this issue with the media on numerous occasions. In a 2014 CNN interview, she talked about the commitment and consequences of staying in a strong and enduring relationship: "But at the same time, you know, I knew, visually, from the depths of my soul, that would be the story. This would be the way people would incessantly and relentlessly write about it. What a B! I can't believe she did that." We do live in a world where emotional intimacy with another human being is a necessary, vital, and inescapable part of making an unforgettable, timeless record. So you wind up in these beautifully intricate situations where you end up in a mesmerizing studio, enveloped in the ethereal waves of music, and maybe, just maybe, you find yourself coexisting in that sacred space with someone who transcends the mere title of a co-writer or producer on the record. They're not just anyone; they become an integral part of your story, intertwining their essence with yours, and thus creating something undeniably magical. Someone you wholeheartedly desire to keep safely and privately tucked away within the sanctuary of hidden whispers. And so you take a real chance, baring your delicate heart and soul, knowing that vulnerability comes with the risk of enduring profound heartbreak. Not just with the ultimate outcome of the record, but with the potential threat of precious moments being exposed in her private haven. This is especially true when her personal life, in particular her relationships - the tender fragments of love and loss that shape her, has long been the subject of many inquisitive questions from the public. It has become a relentless, insatiable curiosity that fuels the intrusive stories and relentless scrutiny within the ever-expanding realm of media. In her personal life, however, Taylor Swift has made it resolutely clear that she yearns to protect the tales inscribed within her songs. When asked about her past stories, she says she genuinely hopes she'll never witness their betrayal and distortion through the merciless lenses of blogs or the vulgarity of tabloids. Distilling her reply, she poetically utters, "I have loved and I have lost it, just like you have loved and lost love, my dear friend," attempting to relinquish the urge to disclose more, simply stating, "I don't really have a story to talk about." The press, with its extensive and sensational history, has thrived on flourishing gossip, particularly when it comes to delving into the intricacies of the romantic lives of female stars. Through all the chaos, Swift has mastered the art of maneuvering her existence, constantly treading the path of performing and promoting her deeply personal romantic melodies to her incredibly diverse and devoutly loyal fans. What then, exists within the intricate and delicate relationship between the enigma of the artist and her relentless pursuit of her craft? Undeniably, Taylor Swift has always strived to keep her life swaddled in a veil of secrecy, while simultaneously packaging and skillfully presenting it to captivate, enthrall, and ultimately amplify the majestic success of her profoundly personal and emotionally resonating love songs. The scale of unwavering attention and captivating intrigue she has ingeniously maintained and cultivated throughout her remarkable journey since those few early dates has not been witnessed since the monumental debut album, fittingly titled "Taylor Swift," was initially released, as if the world was instilled with a flicker of her enigmatic brilliance. The mesmerizing removal of this groundbreaking and genre-defying album from its conventional, genre-focused charts remains one of the central and pivotal considerations of this profoundly thought-provoking and critically engaging article. It all becomes deeply intertwined when interpreting and analyzing the mesmerizingly complex relationship between relentless media attention and the resounding success of an artist's album sales, not to mention their undying influence that transcends time itself.

CHAPTER 8

Chapter 6: Awards and Achievements

In February 2010, Taylor won four Grammy Awards, including Album of the Year for Fearless. The win made her the youngest artist in history to receive the award. That same year, she won Country Song of the Year for "You Belong with Me" and Country Artist of the Year at the Billboard Music Awards. In addition to her four awards, she also won eight of her thirteen Billboard Music Award nominations.

Since 2010, Taylor's accolades have continued to pile. In 2012, she won the Billboard Music Award for Woman of the Year. In 2018, she won the Billboard Music Award for Top Selling Album and Top Female Artist. Taylor currently has 11 Grammy Awards and 34 nominations but has been awarded more than 400 significant industry honors. Many listeners develop a certain respect for the awards themselves over the years. If an artist is beloved by the general public and critics but never receives an award, it must suggest that, as a recording artist, they are extremely underrated. Some musicians may be incredibly famous and well-liked yet have only a single Grammy or no Grammy wins; Taylor has the mindset that if her music has had an emotional effect on her listeners, it is a win in itself. Her 11

Grammy wins from 41 nominations and numerous other industry awards, on the other hand, have solidified her legacy and popularity among her peers. Swift has won many Grammy Awards worth noting, including Best Pop Vocal Album for 1989, Album of the Year for Fearless and 1989, and Best Country Album for Fearless and Speak Now.

Grammy Awards

At the young age of 21, Taylor Swift received the honor to perform her song "Mean" at the 2012 Grammy ceremony. Besides having composed the tune all by herself, she was also wearing a white dress which she designed. For the year 2010, Taylor received Grammy awards for the music of the album "Fearless" at The Prudential Center in Newark, NJ. In 2009, the song "White Horse" was recorded in the category of the best music video. The album "Fearless" entered her in Grammy history when she was honored as the youngest musician ever to have received the CMA (Country Music Association) prize as the Entertainer of the Year.

Ten years later, the fearless singer Taylor Swift has to date won as many as 7 Grammy awards out of 11 nominations, and she sometimes was nominated for two entries in the same category. For the year 2016, she is nominated for 7 entries at the upcoming Grammy Awards to be held in February: 1) Album of the Year; 2) Record of the Year, for "Really Don't Care" sung by Demi Lovato; 3) Best Pop Duo/Group Performance; 4) Best Pop Vocal Album; 5) Song of the Year; 6) Song Written for Visual Media; and 7) Best Song Written for Visual Media. Amongst her nominations, Taylor scored two songs in the category: Song of the Year for "Really Don't Care" and "Shake It Off." Being nominated for 20 categories at the moment implies Taylor Swift is one of the most competitive candidates. She is on her way to beat the most nominated person. If she increases her two additional nominations, then she will be at the top of the list of the most nominated person: Beyonce, with 20. Her Greatest Hits, Volume 1, has received six disc certification multi-platinum sales awards. It is the leading CD for publications up to the fourth of March 2010.

Billboard Music Awards

Taylor can boast 28 wins from 50 nominations over the years at the BBMAs. The first of her 20 trophies was for Digital Artist of the Year won by Taylor Swift in 2011, No.1 Hits Artist, Female Artists, and Overall as well as Top Billboard 200 Artist in 2016. Another big night for Taylor at the BBMAs came in 2013, nine of her 11 nominations resulting in a win. Taylor not only won Top Social Artist (which she shared with Justin Timberlake) and Country Artist (female and overall) but also Artist of the Year. In doing so, Taylor became the first woman to take home the Artist of the Year trophy in history. Two years later Taylor was to take home eight more trophies including Top Artist.

In 2020, Taylor was the biggest winner at the BBMAs. A win for Top Country Artist in 2021 put Taylor's tally of BBMA trophies to date four ahead of Pink and Beyoncé. The only female in front of Taylor is the legendary Whitney Houston with 30 (from 53 nominations). Taylor has won at least one BBMA in 11 different years over her career so far. A unique streak of seven consecutive appearances at the BBMAs where Taylor won at least one award: 2011 – 3 wins from 11 nominations; 2012 – just the one win from eight nominations; 2013 – nine from 11; 2014 – two from 14; 2015 – six from 14; 2018 – two from five; 2019 – two from two; 2020 – 4 wins from four nominations; 2021 – she has picked up 7 more from 10. Obviously should Taylor continue to release albums her chances to win more BBMAs will increase. Taylor is the third biggest winner on night timegol of BBMA trophies!

CHAPTER 9

Chapter 7: Legacy and Future

It is important to analyze a legacy when it comes to a musician or an artist. It becomes clear that the artist has grown past the point of just releasing music on the radio and has become a part of pop culture and has really made an impact on society with their craft. Taylor Swift is one of the biggest legacy artists in the music industry. Her influence spreads out past just her way of words in her music but also in her enablement of her fans and even how the music industry as a whole operates. In the industry today, the Swift way of doing things is the normal way of doing things. That took a lot of power to change the discussion behind the scenes and really shake things up. At the age of 32, Taylor Swift is only just getting started. With her talent and work ethic, the only way to go from here is up.

Taylor Swift is currently working on a few things, all of which will change music as we know it. First of all, she is currently re-recording her hit albums. With each re-released album, she is adding a few never-before-heard tracks for the fans of the albums. She has also acquired rights to her own music and is working with A-List actors Christian Slater, Miles Teller, and Debbi Mazar. She received her Sundance brass ring with "Don't Blame Me," the strip-club song of "Fatal Attraction." She will star in the David O. Russell film "Canterbury Glass" and also will star as Joni Mitchell in the movie "Women of the Spoon," as Chris Collingwood of Fountains of Wayne will also star in that film. She has worked with Christopher Walker for her role in a David Auburn-related acting studio. Her "Swiftstakes" accomplishments with American Express promoting her albums "RED" and "1989" have changed that marketing plan for award shows and album releases as the Taylor Nation Fan Ambassadors are still in action today. She has also hosted television shows and has had a successful partnership with Apple Music.

Enduring Impact on Pop Culture

For the first time ever, Freegal Music user-requested artist Taylor Swift made an appearance on the New York Times Best Seller List with the release of her new book, "Speak Now," in which Swift allows readers an intimate look at a life lived in the limelight. The publisher shared that "Speak Now" is a one-week and Honorable Mention Best Selling book. It's crazy to think that after thirteen years of curating this beautiful love story, Taylor Swift is still underestimated as an artist. After spending years stumbling through a complex web of court battles, transitions, and a pandemic, Swift was freed from her antagonist-driven alter-ego and is now finally getting the commercial success she has long desired. Eight years after her first chart-topping album, people still seem to be underestimating Swift's ability to weave extremely personal, profound, and indeed nosey country tunes. "Lover" was surrounded by followers of "folk-craft" lovers, but the so-called trilogy's highly-anticipated third chapter - now appreciated as a pop tent pole - is where Swift regales us with chapters of pillowy soft, head-voice-led vocals that explore universal experiences. The moment her team first played her new compositions for the public, dubbed "Foreverwinter," ticket sales skyrocketed, leading to additional sold-out vinyl releases. Despite the tragic losses that came with "Intern," fans have fervently waited for the release of a music video that features a montage of clue-spiked bloopers. Every lyric was a hint the narrator dropped along the winding path, and fans, after combing through intimate chapters of theories, awaited a slow buildup to a catchy-come-for-streams chorus. Fans finally got a little magic when Taylor Swift returned to the studio to record her post-pop, genre-straddling tour.

In the summer of 2016, fans pleaded for an emotionally raw bossa nova song inspired by the loss of Jing-Jing the cat, pillow divots, and Taylor's love of all things "fantastical and color." Trading faders for zippers, Taylor flitted to the closet to grab her winter coat and absolutely mastered each intimate musical conversation. Book-end interviews featured irony-infused confidence, somehow laced with awe, and the excitement that her new songs - from the devastation of "Nevermore" to the hope whispered in the title track - even rhyme. While some former naysayers are quick to discredit her meteoric rise to fame as a product of privilege, talent is as talent feels, and "Foreverwinter" feels fearfully talented. When Swift initially pitched these songs to Big Machine Records in the first quarter of 2010, it was her uncanny humility and expectation of a lackluster response that saw her polling advance of fans. Proving herself to be her harshest critic, Swift made a fool of every Weinsteined male she had yet to confront and fell in love with her music. What was originally described as a mediocre pet project of youthful rebellion has ultimately gone on to become one of the best-reviewed releases in modern music. With an ever-evolving sound, Swift's strength lies within a raw, frequent-conversation style of lyrics, paired with infinite productions. "Speak Now" is a top-notch introduction that subverts commercial sibling relationships, "Foreverwinter" is a rural adventurer's go-to, the songs beginning "I Almost Do" that are said to be working progress since its completion are faint whispers of longing that only get louder as they echo into our wildest dreams. Wildlife needs to catch up with Swift's thought process and, best of all, she lives to capture it all in her corner of the world.

Future Projects and Collaborations

Future Projects and Collaborations In revealing the process she undertook to write Red (Taylor's Version), she also leaked plans to re-record more albums and her intention of releasing new music. In October 2020, Taylor began sifting through the backlog of albums she planned to carry out at Republic Records, which includes her favorite song, 2010's 'The Story of Us.' In September 2019, it was reported that Taylor had registered new songs 'Battle' and 'Thirty,' apparently neither of which would have commented to or revised from her current fans. However, these new songs offer a unique and exciting experience for her loyal fans. They eagerly anticipate the release of these tracks, as they long for fresh and captivating music from Taylor. In a surprising twist, Taylor plans to expose the contracts of charities that have obtained wedding streaming rights to distribute a song she will release in 2027. This bold move demonstrates Taylor's commitment to transparency and her desire to support charitable causes. By shedding light on these contracts, she aims to ensure that the revenue generated from her music benefits worthy organizations and causes. Despite the challenges she faces, Taylor remains enthusiastic about her upcoming projects. She is determined to deliver remarkable albums that surpass expectations. Taylor's dedication and talent are unparalleled, and she continues to evolve as an artist. Taylor's creative process for Red highlighted her pride in her voice. She carefully selects each sound and aspect of her music to create a unique and impactful listening experience. Her meticulous approach ensures that each song resonates with listeners on a deeply personal level. As Taylor's career progresses, the possibility of collaborations with other musicians looms. One intriguing suggestion is a Halloween-themed collaboration, which would add an exciting element to her future projects. The thought of Taylor joining forces with another artist to create a haunting and alluring musical experience is electrifying for her fans. Fans eagerly anticipate Taylor's upcoming releases, knowing that she will captivate and inspire audiences worldwide with her incredible talent and dedication. Her future projects are bound to be nothing short of extraordinary. Stay tuned for more updates and thrilling announcements from this iconic singer-songwriter as she continues to write her musical legacy.

CHAPTER 10

Conclusion

In a rapidly advancing era of nine-track technology, the concept of streaming has proven to be unstable and fraught with financial risks for artists who heavily depend on it as their primary source of income. However, Taylor Swift, a remarkably astute entrepreneur, has set her sights on diversifying her portfolio beyond streaming. She has successfully ventured into various realms, including the creation of a clothing line that exudes her signature style. Additionally, she has combined her talents as a book publisher and record label, further establishing herself as a multifaceted businesswoman. Most notably, Taylor Swift has achieved the remarkable feat of persuading Spotify, a prominent platform in the realm of mainstream entertainment, to feature her exceptional songs. This demonstrates her ability to redefine the standards of superstardom and adapt to the modern world as a true CEO overseeing her own thriving company. The triumph of this strategic move grants her the financial freedom to venture into privatizing her work, transforming herself into a modern-day equivalent of Shakespeare. When considering the current landscape, it becomes apparent that Taylor Swift is unmatched in her unrivaled determination, work ethic, influential impact, captivating style, undeniable beauty, remarkable intelligence, ingenious cleverness, and a commanding voice that resonates with the strength of an Iron Lady. Both in her lyrics and musical arrangements, Swift's most distinctive quality lies in her deft ability to seamlessly blend poetic nuance with one-of-a-kind marketing insights that captivate audiences within a single minute. The laudable outcome of this endeavor has brought to light her vulnerabilities and strengths, dreams and desires, hopes and aspirations, as well as unexplored concepts and opportunities, in an era of perpetual change and trends. This introspective journey has served to diversify her artistic identity, aligning her with the insightful observations of Jim Walsh, who aptly described her transformation as a woman who has evolved from being unprepared to live in the present to one who is constantly looking towards the future. In closing, Professor Dr. Heinke's critique of Taylor Swift fails to acknowledge the essence of her artistry, overlooking crucial points such as her intensely introspective approach to songwriting, which resonates on a poetic level, and the sociological significance of her narratives that enthrall an entire field of scholarly study. Moreover, Swift's influences from Nashville, renowned for its captivating storytelling tradition, are paramount in understanding the intricate layers of her music, akin to a compelling plot that thickens as each song unfolds. Finally, the undeniable appeal of Taylor Swift extends its grasp from seven-year-old girls to 77-year-old grandfathers, transcending generations and establishing her as a cultural phenomenon. The incredible versatility of Swift's talents is the bedrock upon which she has cemented her position as a true trailblazer within the music industry, surpassing the constraints imposed by traditional streaming platforms. Her unwavering drive and exceptional business acumen have propelled her far beyond the boundaries of a mere artist, propelling her into the league of an unparalleled cultural icon. Through her various entrepreneurial pursuits, such as her successful clothing line and the establishment of a record label focused on literary works, Swift showcases her endless abilities and strategic navigation of the ever-evolving landscape of entertainment. By skillfully negotiating the inclusion of her songs on Spotify, she not only demonstrates her immense marketability but also solidifies her reputation as a visionary leader who fearlessly adapts to the changing tides of the industry, carrying her own empire forward. This groundbreaking achievement not only underscores her unprecedented financial success but also positions her as a contemporary equivalent of Shakespeare, empowered to shape and redefine her artistic work on her own terms. The dominance of Taylor Swift stretches beyond conventional limits, fueled by an unparalleled fusion of determination, charm, influence, grace, brilliance, wit, and a voice that resounds with the steadfastness of an Iron Lady. Her music is characterized by a unique amalgamation of poetic subtleties and nuanced marketing insights, placing her in a league of her own. With each song, Swift delves deep into introspection, stimulating interpretations that captivate the minds of diverse sociological studies. Her roots in Nashville storytelling enrich her compositions, infusing them with a sense of narrative intrigue that unfolds like an enthralling plot. Whether it is the wide-eyed wonder of young children or the wisdom of elderly grandfathers, her universal appeal remains irrefutable. In stark contrast to the views expressed by Professor Dr. Heinke, Taylor Swift's artistry soars far beyond superficial analysis, delving into the very essence of human emotion and experience. As an extraordinary talent, Taylor Swift continues to captivate audiences, making an indelible impact on the fabric of contemporary music and culture as a whole.

www.ingramcontent.com/pod-product-compliance
Lightning Source LLC
Chambersburg PA
CBHW021356160726
47994CB00007B/2985